D0487209

Stir-fries

Stir-fries

First published in Great Britain in 2000 by
Hamlyn, a division of Octopus Publishing
Group Ltd

This edition published in 2007 by Bounty Books, a
division of Octopus Publishing Group Ltd
2–4 Heron Quays, London E14 4JP

An Hachette Livre UK Company

Copyright © Octopus Publishing Group Ltd 2000

All rights reserved. No part of this work may be
reproduced or utilized in any form or by any
means, electronic or mechanical, including
photocopying, recording or by any information
storage and retrieval system, without the
prior written permission of the publisher

ISBN: 978-0-753716-22-9

A CIP catalogue record for this book is available
from the British Library

Printed and bound in China

Notes

1 Standard level spoon measurements are
used in all recipes.

1 tablespoon = one 15 ml spoon
1 teaspoon = one 5 ml spoon

2 Both imperial and metric measurements
have been given in all recipes. Use one set of
measurements only and not a mixture of both.

3 Measurements for canned food have been
given as a standard metric equivalent.

4 Eggs should be medium unless otherwise
stated. The Department of Health advises that
eggs should not be consumed raw. This book
may contain dishes made with lightly cooked
eggs. It is prudent for more vulnerable people,
such as pregnant and nursing mothers,
invalids, the elderly, babies and young
children, to avoid uncooked or lightly cooked
dishes made with eggs. Once prepared, these
dishes should be used immediately.

5 Milk should be full fat unless otherwise
stated.

6 Poultry should be cooked thoroughly.
To test if poultry is cooked, pierce the flesh
through the thickest part with a skewer or
fork – the juices should run clear, never pink
or red.

7 Fresh herbs should be used unless otherwise stated. If unavailable, use dried herbs as
an alternative but halve the quantities stated.

8 Pepper should be freshly ground black
pepper unless otherwise stated; season
according to taste.

9 Ovens should be preheated to the specified
temperature – if using a fan-assisted oven,
 follow the manufacturer's instructions for
adjusting the time and the temperature.

10 Do not re-freeze a dish that has been
frozen previously.

11 This book includes dishes made with nuts
and nut derivatives. It is advisable for
customers with known allergic reactions to
nuts and nut derivatives and those who may
be potentially vulnerable to these allergies,
such as pregnant and nursing mothers,
invalids, the elderly, babies and children,
to avoid dishes made with nuts and nut oils.
It is also prudent to check the labels of
pre-prepared ingredients for the possible
inclusion of nut derivatives.

12 Vegetarians should look for the 'V' symbol
on a cheese to ensure it is made with
vegetarian rennet. There are vegetarian forms
of Parmesan, feta, Cheddar, Cheshire, red
Leicester, dolcelatte and many goats' cheeses,
among others.

Surprisingly filling, rice and noodle based dishes excel as main courses or special side dishes. Try the tantalising Coconut Rice with Fish and Peas on its own and serve Spicy Fried Rice with one of the meat dishes.

Combining two of the most popular trends in cooking - fast and healthy - these fresh and delicious dishes will be a hit with family and friends as a main course or accompaniment.

Extremely versatile and good for you, fish is a superb main ingredient for midweek meals for the family and stylish entertaining alike.

Feel like chicken, turkey or duck tonight? Try one of these yummy recipes such as Ginger Chicken with Honey or Sesame Marinated Turkey and get your tastebuds dancing!

From the tangy Sweet & Sour Pork to the hot and spicy Szechuan Shredded Beef these fabulous and hearty dishes can be whipped up anytime of the year with great success.

contents

6

introduction

Stir-frying is one of the simplest and healthiest of cooking methods. Speed is its real advantage, turning ingredients into an exciting dish in minutes while preserving their excellent food value. The technique usually brings the wok and Chinese food, in particular, to mind, but its use is far more widespread. A fabulous variety of South-east Asian dishes are stir-fried to perfection.

The Western equivalent, sautéing, is a similar method of cooking over high heat in a large pan (the classic sauté pan is slightly deeper than the usual frying pan), tossing and turning the food vigorously. Generous lumps of lard or butter are traditional for sautéing, which does not have a reputation for being healthy and is now usually replaced by stir-frying. Modern cooks have transformed oriental stir-frying into a versatile international technique for ingredients and seasonings as diverse as their countries of origin.

Equipment

A wok is the traditional pan for stir-frying, and there are many different types of woks available in stores today. Some are sold as complete sets with chopsticks, lids and various accessories.

Woks and Pans

A wok is not essential, but you will need a large pan to allow plenty of room for combining the ingredients (many stir-fries are one-pot meals) without having them flying over the top as you stir and cook.

Woks The traditional carbon steel wok is designed for cooking over an open brazier – its thin metal dome sits neatly in a frame over a fierce outdoor fire or gas burner and conducts heat well, so it heats rapidly and the heats spreads out well. A wide top and deep sloping sides are ideal for shaking, tossing and turning ingredients, ensuring they fall back into the bottom, rather than out over the top. Used daily, cleaned with fresh oil and paper (with salt for scouring the metal), carbon steel is fine, but if it is not in frequent use and washed without being seasoned (heated with oil) it rusts. There is a good choice of woks that can be washed and stored without oiling, some with slightly flatter bases for optimum cooking on the average gas or electric hob. Look for a wok with a domed, close-fitting lid which is useful for retaining moisture when simmering (often used briefly after stir-frying to complete the cooking) or for steaming food placed on a rack in the wok.

Frying pans A large frying pan with fairly deep sides can be used. A classic sauté pan designed to withstand high temperatures and with deep, straight sides is ideal. A large skillet – a deep, straight-sided and covered frying pan – can be more practical than some woks as its flat base heats quickly and evenly and the deep sides allow plenty of room for tossing ingredients.

Saucepans A large saucepan is practical if it has a wide base that conducts heat well and withstands high temperatures without burning. Do not be tempted to cook

'I feel a recipe is only a theme, which an intelligent cook can play each time with a variation.'

Madame Benoit

large amounts in a small or medium saucepan as the ingredients will not be in contact with the bottom and they will not fry sufficiently quickly.

Stainless steel A good-quality stainless steel wok or pan with a base manufactured to conduct heat well can be used over high heat and the sides will also become hot. Follow the manufacturer's instructions for years of excellent use from this type of wok or pan.

Non-stick finishes These can be problematic as many non-stick surfaces do not respond well to being heated empty and they do not last well when used over high heat. Non-stick woks do conduct heat properly, but stir-frying is often carried out over a high heat and this reduces the life of the coating. Metal utensils are not suitable, but there are plenty of alternatives with specialist finishes.

Oils and Fats

Stir-frying is rapid, therefore ingredients must require minimum cooking and with-stand the vigorous stirring. Firm fish and shellfish; lean and tender cuts of meat; chicken, turkey and duck breast (without fat); and all sorts of vegetables and fruit are ideal. Cooked rice and noodles can also be stir-fried briefly. All ingredients should be in prime condition as quick cooking emphasises any shortfall in quality.

Basic vegetable oil is versatile and suitable for most ingredients; groundnut oil withstands high heat and is ideal for rapidly browning and crisping strips of poultry or meat; olive oil does not withstand high temperatures, but it can be used for briefly stir-frying over less-fierce heat.

Sesame oil is popular in oriental dishes, but overheats rapidly and is rarely used as the main oil in which to cook food, but is more often added as a flavouring. It can be combined with vegetable oil for frying or added towards the end of cooking.

Butter is not used in oriental cooking, but is good with vegetables and other ingredients in Western-style dishes. Ideally, it should be clarified (melted and cooked gently until its water content has evaporated, then strained to remove any sediment) so that it can be heated to a high temperature without burning. A little butter with olive oil is a well-balanced option.

Lard is a classic fat for oriental as well as Western dishes and can be heated to a high temperature. However, it is no longer popular for everyday cooking. If it is not hot enough, lard will give a greasy result.

Preparation

All ingredients must be prepared or assembled before starting to stir-fry. Minutes spent finding seasoning or spice in the middle of stir-frying can result in ingredients that overcook, becoming juicy and soft rather than retaining a crisp, fresh texture. Everything should be cut into pieces that cook quickly and evenly. Thin slices, fine strips, small cubes and dice are typical. Tender foods that cook very fast (and may overcook) can be cut into slightly thicker slices, larger chunks or fingers, especially when combined with firm ingredients.

The Technique

Before adding any ingredients, the oil must be hot. Depending on its type, the pan can be heated empty until very hot before adding oil. This is useful for meat as the combination of a very hot pan and oil seals the pieces fast before they give up any juices that can spoil the stir-frying. For most dishes, it is usually best to heat the oil in the pan, starting over a moderate heat so that the pan can heat thoroughly.

Adding ingredients The food is rarely cooked together in one batch. Ingredients that require longest are stir-fried first, until part cooked, then they are pushed to one side of the pan as the remaining food is added in stages according to how long it takes to cook. Ingredients can also be stir-fried, then removed from the pan to be returned when the remainder of the dish has been assembled.

Stirring and turning Simply stirring ingredients around is not enough: the food should be moved from the edge of the pan towards the middle using a turning and stirring motion. This ensures that all the pieces are evenly cooked on all sides.

Serving Stir-fried dishes are often served freshly cooked. Have bowls or serving dishes warmed and make sure everyone is ready to eat before you begin cooking. Many one-pot meals can be served straight from the pan (if it is smart enough), especially a wok as the narrow base will fit over a candle warmer and the wide top allows plenty of space for serving the food at the table.

spicy fried rice with red chillies ●
fried rice with ham & bean sprouts ●
special egg fried rice ●
coconut rice with fish & peas ●
creamy rice with fish ●
pineapple fried rice ●
ten-variety fried rice ●
chow mein ●
singapore noodles ●
egg noodles in yellow bean & chilli sauce ●
thai fried noodles ●
noodles with chicken & prawns ●

oodles of rice & noodles

12

spicy fried rice with red chillies

1 Rinse the rice in a sieve under cold running water and drain well. Place the rice in a saucepan, pour in the water, and add salt to taste. Bring to the boil, stir once, cover and simmer for 15–20 minutes or until the water has been absorbed. Remove from the heat and set aside in the covered pan.

2 Heat the oil in a wok or frying pan, add the shallots or onion and chillies and stir-fry for 1–3 minutes. Add the pork, beef or bacon and stir-fry for 3 minutes.

3 Add the rice, soy sauce and tomato purée. Stir-fry for 5–8 minutes, then season with salt to taste.

4 Transfer the rice mixture to a warmed serving dish or bowls. Garnish with fried onion rings, strips of omelette, coriander leaves and the cucumber slices. Serve at once.

375 g (12 oz) long-grain rice

750 ml (1¼ pints) water

2 tablespoons sunflower oil

4 shallots or 1 onion, thinly sliced

2 red chillies, deseeded and thinly sliced

50 g (2 oz) lean boneless pork, beef or bacon, finely diced

1 tablespoon light soy sauce

1 teaspoon tomato purée

salt

To Garnish:

fried onion rings

1 thin omelette, made with 1 egg, cut into strips

coriander leaves

cucumber slices

Serves 4

Preparation time: 15 minutes

Cooking time: about 25–30 minutes

fried rice with ham & bean sprouts

1 Rinse the rice in a sieve under cold running water and drain well. Place the rice in a saucepan, pour in the water and add salt to taste. Bring to the boil, stir once, cover and simmer for 15–20 minutes or until the water has been absorbed. Turn the rice into a sieve and rinse it under cold running water, then set it aside to drain.

2 Heat the oil in a wok or frying pan over a moderate heat and stir-fry the spring onions and garlic for about 2 minutes. Add the rice and stir well. Cook gently, stirring continuously as the rice heats through. Stir in the ham and soy sauce.

3 Beat the eggs thoroughly, adding salt and pepper to taste. Pour the eggs into the rice mixture in a thin stream, stirring all the time. Add the bean sprouts and continue cooking, stirring continuously, until the eggs are set and all the ingredients are hot. Serve at once.

375 g (12 oz) long-grain rice

1.2 litres (2 pints) water

2 tablespoons sunflower oil

2 spring onions, finely chopped

1 garlic clove, crushed

175 g (6 oz) cooked ham, diced

2 tablespoons light soy sauce

2 eggs

250 g (8 oz) bean sprouts, rinsed and drained

salt and pepper

Serves 4

Preparation time: 15 minutes

Cooking time: 8–10 minutes

■ The rice can be cooked in advance, cooled and chilled. This is also a quick, tasty dish for using leftover cooked rice.

special egg fried rice

1 Lightly beat the eggs with 1 teaspoon of the spring onions and a pinch of salt. Heat 1 tablespoon of the oil in a wok or heavy frying pan and add the eggs. Stir constantly until the eggs are lightly set and scrambled, then transfer them to a bowl and set the mixture aside.

2 Heat the remaining oil in the wok or pan. Add the prawns, meat, bamboo shoots, peas and remaining spring onions. Stir-fry briskly for about 1 minute, then add the soy sauce and stir-fry for 2–3 minutes.

3 Add the rice to the wok. Replace the scrambled eggs and add salt to taste. Stir well to break up the scrambled eggs and thoroughly reheat and separate the grains of rice. Serve hot, garnished with spring onions.

2–3 eggs

2 spring onions, finely chopped

3 tablespoons vegetable oil

125 g (4 oz) cooked, peeled prawns

125 g (4 oz) cooked meat, such as chicken or pork, diced

50 g (2 oz) canned bamboo shoots, diced

4 tablespoons fresh or frozen peas, cooked

1 tablespoon light soy sauce

375–500 g (12–16 oz) cold, cooked rice

salt

chopped spring onions, to garnish

Serves 4

Preparation time: 15 minutes

Cooking time: 8–10 minutes

16

coconut rice with fish & peas

1 Melt half the butter in a large frying pan. Stir in the coriander, turmeric, cinnamon and pepper, then add the fish and stir-fry for 1–2 minutes until golden on all sides. Transfer the fish to a bowl using a slotted spoon, taking care not to break up the pieces. Set aside.

2 Melt the remaining butter in the pan and fry the onion and garlic for 5 minutes. Add the rice, stir well until all the grains are glossy, then add the tomatoes, stock and coconut milk. Bring to the boil, cover and simmer for 15 minutes.

3 Stir in the peas, taste and adjust the seasoning, if necessary, and arrange the fish on top of the rice. Cover with foil and then the lid and cook for 5 minutes. Leave to stand for a further 5 minutes without removing the foil and lid.

4 Transfer the rice mixture to a warmed serving dish. Scatter the coriander or parsley over the top and add sprigs or coriander (if using), then serve immediately.

25 g (1 oz) butter

1 teaspoon ground coriander

½ teaspoon turmeric

½ teaspoon ground cinnamon

½ teaspoon pepper

375 g (12 oz) monkfish or skinless cod fillet, cut into bite-sized pieces

1 onion, chopped

1 garlic clove, crushed

250 g (8 oz) long-grain rice

400 g (13 oz) can chopped tomatoes

300 ml (½ pint) vegetable stock

200 ml (7 fl oz) coconut milk

125 g (4 oz) frozen peas, thawed

To Garnish:

1 tablespoon chopped coriander or parsley

sprigs of coriander (optional)

Serves 4

Preparation time: 10 minutes

Cooking time: 31–32 minutes

creamy rice with fish

1 Rinse the rice in a sieve under cold running water, then drain well. Bring 600 ml (1 pint) of the chicken stock to the boil in a large saucepan. Add the rice, cover and cook for 15–20 minutes over a low heat, stirring occasionally. The rice should absorb most of the stock. Add the remaining 1 litre (1¾ pints) stock, bring back to the boil, then remove the pan from the heat.

2 Heat the oil in a wok, add the garlic and stir-fry until just golden. Use a slotted spoon to remove the garlic and set it aside. Add the cod and stir-fry for 4–6 minutes, adding the 2 tablespoons stock, if necessary, to prevent the fish from sticking.

3 As soon as the cod is cooked, add it to the rice together with the fish sauce and pepper. Mix well and transfer to a serving dish.

4 Garnish the rice mixture with shredded spring onion, chopped celery and the reserved fried garlic. Serve immediately.

175 g (6 oz) long-grain rice

1.6 litres (2¾ pints), plus 2 tablespoons, chicken stock

3 tablespoons vegetable oil

1 tablespoon finely chopped garlic

500 g (1 lb) cod fillet, thinly sliced

2 tablespoons fish sauce (nam pla)

1 teaspoon freshly ground black pepper

To Garnish:

2 spring onions, shredded

2 celery sticks, very finely chopped

Sérves 4
Preparation time: 10 minutes
Cooking time: 30 minutes

pineapple fried rice

1 Rinse the rice in a sieve under cold running water and drain well. Place the rice in a saucepan, pour in the water and add salt to taste. Bring to the boil, stir once, cover and simmer for 15–20 minutes or until the water has been absorbed. Turn the rice into a sieve and rinse it under cold running water, then set it aside and leave to drain.

2 Heat the oil in a wok. Add the garlic and stir-fry until just golden. Add the ham, carrot, raisins, green and red pepper, fish sauce and sugar. Stir-fry for 5 minutes.

3 Add the rice and pineapple. Season the mixture with pepper and stir-fry for a further 5 minutes. Garnish the fried rice with chopped coriander and serve immediately.

250 g (8 oz) long-grain rice

750 ml (1¼ pints) water

4 tablespoons vegetable oil

1 garlic clove, crushed

125 g (4 oz) cooked ham, cubed

1 carrot, diced

4 tablespoons raisins

¼ green pepper, cored, deseeded and diced

¼ red pepper, cored, deseeded and diced

4 tablespoons fish sauce (nam pla)

1 tablespoon sugar

4 pineapple rings, diced

salt and pepper

2 tablespoons chopped coriander, to garnish

Serves 4
Preparation time: 10 minutes
Cooking time: 25–30 minutes

ten-variety fried rice

1 Rinse the rice in a sieve under cold running water and drain well. Place the rice in a saucepan, pour in the water and add salt to taste. Bring to the boil, stir once, cover and simmer for 15–20 minutes or until the water has been absorbed. Turn the rice into a sieve and rinse it under cold water, then set it aside to drain.

2 Meanwhile, heat 1 tablespoon of the oil in a wok. Add the egg, swirling it around to form a thick skin in the bottom of the wok. When set, turn the omelette out on to a board and leave to cool. Roll up the omelette tightly, slice it finely and set it aside. Mix the sauce ingredients in a bowl.

3 Heat another 1 tablespoon of the oil in the wok, then add the chicken and pork. Stir-fry for 4 minutes over a high heat, until lightly browned. Transfer to a bowl and set aside.

4 Add and heat the remaining oil, then stir-fry the red pepper, spring onions, garlic and chillies for 2–3 minutes or until softened.

5 Stir in the tomatoes and cooked rice, then replace the chicken, pork and their juices. Pour in the sauce and toss well over high heat until hot. Fold in the prawns and crab meat and heat through, shaking the wok occasionally. Top with omelette and garnish with cucumber strips.

175 g (6 oz) long-grain rice

600 ml (1 pint) water

3½ tablespoons vegetable oil

1 egg, beaten

175 g (6 oz) boneless, skinless chicken breast, finely sliced

125–175 g (4–6 oz) pork fillet, finely sliced

1 red pepper, cored, deseeded and finely chopped

4 spring onions, finely sliced

2 garlic cloves, crushed

3 green chillies, deseeded and finely chopped

3 tomatoes, chopped

125 g (4 oz) cooked, peeled prawns

125 g (4 oz) white crab meat, flaked

salt

cucumber strips, to garnish

Sauce:

150 ml (¼ pint) fish stock

2 tablespoons soy sauce

1 tablespoon caster sugar

2 teaspoons lemon juice

2 teaspoons fish sauce (nam pla)

Serves 3–4

Preparation time: 25 minutes

Cooking time: 35 minutes

chow mein

1 Cook the egg noodles in boiling, salted water for about 5 minutes, or until tender but still firm to the bite (al dente). Cook spaghettini in the same way, allowing slightly longer, according to the packet instructions. Drain the pasta well and rinse under cold running water until cool, then set aside.

2 Heat 3 tablespoons of the oil in a wok. Add the onion, meat, mangetout or beans and the bean sprouts, and stir-fry for about 1 minute. Season the mixture well, stir briefly, then use a slotted spoon to transfer the mixture to a bowl and keep hot.

3 Heat the remaining oil in the wok and add the spring onions and the noodles. Replace about half of the meat and vegetable mixture. Add the soy sauce, then stir-fry for 1–2 minutes, or until completely heated through.

4 Transfer the mixture to a warmed serving dish, top with all of the remaining meat and vegetable mixture and sprinkle with the sesame oil or chilli sauce (or both if liked). Serve immediately.

500 g (1 lb) egg noodles or spaghettini

4 tablespoons vegetable oil

1 onion, thinly sliced

125 g (4 oz) cooked meat, such as pork, chicken or ham, finely shredded

125 g (4 oz) mangetout or French beans

125 g (4 oz) bean sprouts

2–3 spring onions, finely shredded

2 tablespoons light soy sauce

1 tablespoon sesame oil or chilli sauce

salt

Serves 4

Preparation time: 15 minutes

Cooking time: 15–18 minutes

■ Literally translated, chow mein means 'stir-fried noodles'. This popular, versatile dish was created by Chinese immigrants in the United States using whatever ingredients they had. Try different combinations of meat and vegetables with the noodles to vary the dish.

1 Cook the noodles in boiling water for 2 minutes. Drain well.

2 Bring the water to the boil in a pan and cook the pork, prawns and squid together for 5 minutes. Drain, reserving the cooking liquid.

3 Heat the oil in a wok or frying pan and fry the garlic until golden. Add the bean sprouts and noodles, increase the heat, and stir-fry for 2 minutes.

4 Add the pork mixture, the soy sauces, pepper and chives, and stir-fry for a further 1 minute. Push the mixture to one side of the pan and add the eggs to the space. Cook them for 1 minute, stirring, then stir in the reserved cooking liquid.

5 Bring to the boil and cook for 2 minutes, stirring well. Transfer to a warmed serving dish and serve.

375 g (12 oz) fine egg noodles

575 ml (18 fl oz) water

125 g (4 oz) lean pork, cut into 5 cm (2 inch) strips

75 g (3 oz) uncooked prawns, shelled

75 g (3 oz) prepared squid, sliced

4 tablespoons sunflower oil

2 garlic cloves, crushed

75 g (3 oz) bean sprouts

1 tablespoon light soy sauce

1 tablespoon dark soy sauce

½ teaspoon pepper

1 bunch of chives, snipped

2 eggs

Serves 4
Preparation time: 15 minutes
Cooking time: 14–18 minutes

singapore noodles

egg noodles in yellow bean & chilli sauce

1 Cook the egg noodles in boiling, salted water for about 5 minutes, or until tender but still firm to the bite (al dente). Cook spaghettini in the same way, allowing slightly longer according to the packet instructions. Drain the pasta well.

2 Mix the yellow bean paste, chilli sauce and garlic, then set this sauce aside. Heat the oil in a wok or large frying pan over high heat. Add the peppers, onion and bean sprouts and stir-fry for 2 minutes.

3 Add the noodles to the wok and stir in the sauce. Heat through, turning the pasta carefully, then taste for seasoning and transfer to a warmed serving dish.

375 g (12 oz) egg noodles or spaghettini

3 tablespoons yellow bean paste

2 teaspoons chilli sauce

1 garlic clove, crushed

3 tablespoons vegetable oil

2 green peppers, cored, deseeded and cut into thin strips

1 medium onion, thinly sliced

150 g (5 oz) bean sprouts

salt

Serves 4

Preparation time: 10 minutes

Cooking time: 10 minutes

■ Bean sauces are popular in Chinese cooking. Yellow bean sauce, made from salted soya beans, garlic, soy sauce, vinegar, sugar and seasoning, is milder than black bean sauce.

thai fried
noodles

1 Heat 2 tablespoons of the oil in
   a wok. Stir-fry the tofu until brown
on all sides. Then add the garlic, the
noodles, carrot, vinegar, soy sauce and
water, stirring continuously.

2 Push the mixture to one side
   of the wok and add the eggs to
the space. Break the yolks and stir
the eggs, gradually incorporating the
noodle mixture.

3 Pour the remaining oil down the
   side of the wok and add the
sugar, spring onions and pepper. Cook
for 2–3 minutes, stirring and shaking
the wok continuously.

4 Heap the noodle mixture on to
   a plate. Sprinkle the peanuts on
top and serve with the bean sprouts
and spring onion halves.

3 tablespoons groundnut oil

175 g (6 oz) ready-fried tofu (bean
curd), diced

1 tablespoon chopped garlic

125 g (4 oz) bean thread noodles,
soaked and drained

25 g (1 oz) carrot, grated

2 tablespoons distilled white vinegar
or Chinese rice vinegar

2 tablespoons soy sauce

100 ml (3½ fl oz) water

2 eggs

3 teaspoons sugar

2 spring onions, sliced

¼ teaspoon pepper

To Serve:

1 tablespoon crushed roasted
peanuts

125 g (4 oz) bean sprouts

1 spring onion, halved lengthways

Serves 2

Preparation time: 15 minutes,
plus soaking

Cooking time: 20–25 minutes

noodles with chicken & prawns

1 Soak the dried mushrooms in hot water for 35–40 minutes. Meanwhile, cook the egg noodles in boiling, salted water for 5 minutes, or until tender but still firm to the bite (al dente). Drain the noodles and divide them between 6 bowls. Keep warm.

2 Drain the mushrooms in a sieve. Discard any tough stalks and thinly slice the mushroom caps.

3 Heat the oil in a wok. Add the chicken, garlic and ginger, and stir-fry over a moderate to high heat for 2–3 minutes. Add the spring onions and mushrooms and stir-fry for about 2 minutes.

4 Stir in the prawns, soy sauce, rice wine or sherry, stock and salt to taste. Bring to the boil over a high heat, then reduce the heat and simmer for 5 minutes. Blend the cornflour to a smooth paste with a little cold water, then stir this into the chicken mixture and cook, stirring, until the sauce boils and thickens.

5 Pour the chicken and prawns over the noodles, sprinkle with the shredded ham and serve.

25 g (1 oz) dried shiitake mushrooms

500 g (1 lb) egg noodles

2 tablespoons groundnut oil

175 g (6 oz) boneless, skinless chicken breast, diced

1 garlic clove, crushed

2 slices of fresh root ginger, peeled and chopped

4 spring onions, thinly sliced diagonally into 1 cm (½ inch) pieces

175 g (6 oz) uncooked prawns, peeled

2 tablespoons soy sauce

2 tablespoons Chinese rice wine or dry sherry

900 ml (1½ pints) chicken stock

2 tablespoons cornflour

50 g (2 oz) cooked ham, shredded

salt

Serves 6

Preparation time: 20 minutes, plus soaking

Cooking time: 20 minutes

vital vegetables

28

crispy tofu in tomato sauce

1 Heat the oil in a wok or a deep frying pan. Add the tofu and stir-fry until it is golden brown. Remove from the oil with a slotted spoon and set the tofu aside.

2 Place the tomatoes in a medium saucepan with the stock, fish sauce, salt and sugar. Bring to the boil, reduce the heat and simmer gently for 15–20 minutes.

3 Add the tofu and simmer for a further 10–15 minutes. The sauce should be thick when ready. Serve immediately, garnished with shredded spring onion.

■ For a totally vegetarian dish, use vegetable stock and either totally omit the fish sauce or substitute with a seaweed-based seasoning which is available from health food stores.

oil, for frying

6 pieces of tofu (bean curd), halved and cut into bite-size triangles

3 large tomatoes, skinned, deseeded and finely chopped

150 ml (¼ pint) vegetable or chicken stock

1 tablespoon fish sauce (nam pla) (optional)

pinch of salt

⅓ teaspoon sugar

2 shredded spring onions, to garnish

Serves 4

Preparation time: 15 minutes

Cooking time: about 40 minutes

three bean stir-fry

1 Heat the wok until hot. Add the oil and heat over a moderate heat until hot. Add the onion and garlic and stir-fry over a gentle heat until the onion has softened slightly.

2 Add the 3 types of beans and increase the heat to high. Toss well to mix then add the passatta or creamed tomatoes a little at a time and stir-fry after each addition until evenly combined with the beans.

3 Add the tomato purée, Worcestershire sauce and sugar; then boil until reduced, stirring the mixture constantly. Remove from the heat, stir in the parsley and salt and pepper to taste. Garnish with parlsey sprigs and serve immediately.

2 tablespoons vegetable oil

1 onion, finely chopped

2 garlic cloves, crushed

425 g (14 oz) can borlotti beans, drained and rinsed

425 g (14 oz) can red kidney beans, drained and rinsed

425 g (14 oz) can cannellini beans, drained and rinsed

425 g (14 oz) can passatta or creamed tomatoes

2 tablespoons tomato purée

2 teaspoons Worcestershire sauce

1 teaspoon granulated sugar

4 tablespoons chopped parsley

salt and pepper

parsley sprigs, to garnish

Serves 4

Preparation time: 15 minutes

Cooking time: about 20 minutes

1 Wash the bean sprouts in a basin of cold water, discarding the husks from the beans and any other particles that float to the surface. Drain well.

2 Heat the oil in a wok until it is smoking hot. Add the spring onion, then add the beans and stir a few times. Add the bean sprouts and stir-fry for 30 seconds.

3 Add the sugar and salt to taste, and stir-fry for a further 1 minute. Transfer to a serving dish, sprinkle with the sesame oil and serve immediately.

500 g (1 lb) bean sprouts

3–4 tablespoons sunflower oil

1 spring onion, finely chopped

250 g (8 oz) dwarf French beans, halved

1 teaspoon sugar

1 teaspoon sesame oil

salt

Serves 4
Preparation time: 10 minutes
Cooking time: 3–4 minutes

bean sprout & green bean stir-fry

■ Fresh bean sprouts are best, preferably bought on the day you plan to use them, as the canned vegetables do not have the same crunchy texture.

aubergines in fragrant sauce

1 Heat the oil for deep-frying in a deep wok or large saucepan to 180–190°C (350–375°F) or until a day-old cube of bread browns in 30 seconds. Deep-fry the aubergine for 1–2 minutes, until golden. Use a slotted spoon to remove the aubergines from the pan and place them on kitchen paper to drain.

2 Carefully pour the oil out of the wok, leaving about 1 tablespoon and reheat this. Quickly stir-fry the spring onions, ginger and garlic. Add and stir-fry the pork, if using, then stir in the soy sauce, sherry and chilli sauce. Add the aubergine wedges and stir-fry for 1–2 minutes.

3 Mix the cornflour to a smooth paste with a little water and then stir it into the aubergine mixture. Bring to the boil, stirring, and cook briefly until the sauce thickens. Serve immediately.

vegetable oil, for deep-frying

250 g (8 oz) aubergines, peeled and cut into small, thick wedges

2 spring onions, chopped

1 slice of fresh root ginger, peeled and chopped

1 garlic clove, chopped

125 g (4 oz) pork fillet, cut into fine strips (optional)

1 tablespoon soy sauce

1 tablespoon dry sherry

2 teaspoons chilli sauce

2 tablespoons cornflour

Serves 2–3

Preparation time: 15 minutes

Cooking time: about 10 minutes

stir-fried green beans

1 Heat the oil in a wok or large frying pan. Add the garlic, shallots and ginger. Stir-fry over a moderate heat for 1 minute. Stir in the chilli with salt to taste, and continue stir-frying for 30 seconds.

2 Add the green beans and cashew nuts and toss well to combine the ingredients. Stir-fry quickly for 1 minute to brown the cashew nuts.

3 Stir in the stock, sherry, soy sauce, vinegar and sugar and bring to the boil. Reduce the heat slightly and cook, stirring, for about 4 minutes, until the beans are cooked and the liquid has thickened. Taste and adjust the seasoning if necessary, then serve immediately sprinkled with plenty of black pepper.

3 tablespoons oil

2 garlic cloves, crushed

2 shallots, thinly sliced

1 slice of fresh root ginger, peeled and chopped

1 red chilli, deseeded and finely chopped

500 g (1 lb) green beans, cut into 5cm (2 inch) lengths

50 g (2 oz) unsalted cashew nuts

125 ml (4 fl oz) vegetable or chicken stock

2 tablespoons dry sherry

1 tablespoon light soy sauce

1 teaspoon vinegar

1 teaspoon sugar

salt and pepper

Serves 4
Preparation time: 10 minutes
Cooking time: 7–8 minutes

■ Shallots have a slightly milder flavour than onion; if they are not available, try using $1/2$ mild white or red salad onion instead of the usual full-flavoured and fairly small cooking onions.

stir-fried vegetables

1 Soak the dried mushrooms in warm water for 25–30 minutes. Drain and squeeze the mushrooms, then discard the hard stalks and thinly slice the caps. If using fresh mushrooms, wash and slice them.

2 Heat the oil in a wok or heavy frying pan until it is smoking hot. Reduce the heat and stir-fry the Chinese leaves and carrots briskly for 30 seconds.

3 Add the beans and mushrooms and continue stir-frying for about 30 seconds. Add the salt and sugar. Toss the vegetables until they are well blended. Stir in the soy sauce and cook for a further 1 minute. Transfer the mixture to a warmed serving dish and serve immediately.

5–6 dried shiitake mushrooms or 50 g (2 oz) button mushrooms

4 tablespoons vegetable oil

250 g (8 oz) Chinese leaves, thinly sliced diagonally

175 g (6 oz) carrots, thinly sliced diagonally

125 g (4 oz) French beans, halved if long

1 teaspoon salt

1 teaspoon sugar

1 tablespoon light soy sauce

Serves 3–4

Preparation time: 10 minutes, plus soaking

Cooking time: 3–4 minutes

■ Fresh shiitake mushrooms are usually available from larger supermarkets and they can be used instead of the dried mushrooms. Trim and slice them as for fresh button mushrooms.

36

stir-fried mixed mushrooms

1 Soak the dried mushrooms in warm water for 25–30 minutes. Drain and squeeze the mushrooms, then discard the hard stalks and thinly slice the caps.

2 Heat the oil in a wok or large frying pan over a moderate heat. Add the ginger, spring onions and the garlic, and stir-fry for 5–10 seconds. Then add the dried mushrooms and button mushrooms, and continue stir-frying for 5 minutes.

3 Add the straw mushrooms, chilli bean sauce or chilli powder, sherry, soy sauce, stock, sugar, salt and sesame oil. Mix well and then stir-fry for a further 5 minutes. Serve the mushrooms immediately.

50 g (2 oz) dried shiitake mushrooms

1 tablespoon oil

1 teaspoon finely chopped fresh root ginger

2 spring onions, finely chopped

1 garlic clove, crushed

250 g (8 oz) button mushrooms, halved or quartered if large

200 g (7 oz) can straw mushrooms, drained

1 teaspoon chilli bean sauce or chilli powder

2 teaspoons dry sherry

2 teaspoons dark soy sauce

1 tablespoon vegetable or chicken stock

pinch of sugar

pinch of salt

1 teaspoon sesame oil

Serves 4

Preparation time: 5 minutes, plus soaking

Cooking time: 10 minutes

stir-fried vegetable omelette

1 Heat the oil in a wok or frying pan. Stir-fry the onion until softened. Add the garlic, potatoes, pepper and broccoli, and stir-fry for 6 minutes, or until tender but still crisp. (Add a little water if the vegetables start to stick to the pan.)

2 Stir in the tomatoes and chopped cucumber, then spread the mixture out flat. Pour the eggs over the vegetables, stir well and flatten the mixture again. Cook, without stirring, until the eggs begin to set, then place the pan under a preheated hot grill until the top of the omelette has set.

3 Cut the omelette into wedges. Sprinkle with parsley and pepper, and serve immediately.

■ Vary the vegetables according to the season – for example, try mushrooms, cooked and drained spinach, bean sprouts or mangetout. Add a little chopped fresh dill, if liked.

1 tablespoon sunflower oil

1 onion, finely chopped

1 garlic clove, crushed

2 potatoes, quartered and finely sliced

½ green or red pepper, cored, deseeded and finely chopped

4–6 broccoli florets

3 tomatoes, sliced

¼ cucumber, chopped

5–6 large eggs, beaten

1 heaped teaspoon chopped parsley

pepper

Serves 4–6

Preparation time: 5 minutes

Cooking time: 10 minutes

38

chinese cabbage in sweet & sour sauce

1 Heat the oil and butter in a wok or a large frying pan. Add the bok choy and sprinkle with the salt. Stir-fry for 2 minutes, then reduce the heat and simmer gently for 5–6 minutes.

2 Meanwhile, in a small saucepan, mix the cornflour to a smooth paste with the water, then stir in the remaining sauce ingredients. Bring to the boil, reduce the heat and simmer for 4–5 minutes, stirring continuously, until the sauce thickens.

3 Transfer the cabbage to a serving dish and pour the sauce over and serve immediately.

■ Bok choy is widely available at greengrocers and supermarkets. It has a loose head of deep green leaves with short, wide white stalks. The leaves are crisp and juicy in texture, with a mild mustard flavour. Swiss chard can be used instead.

3 tablespoons vegetable oil

15 g (½ oz) butter

2 heads of bok choy, shredded

1 teaspoon salt

Sauce:

1½ tablespoons cornflour

5 tablespoons water

1½ tablespoons soy sauce

2½ tablespoons sugar

3½ tablespoons vinegar

3½ tablespoons orange juice

2½ tablespoons tomato purée

1½ tablespoons Chinese wine or dry sherry

Serves 4

Preparation time: 5 minutes

Cooking time: 11–13 minutes

fishing for compliments

king prawn & coconut curry

1 Purée all the ingredients for the spice paste in a blender or spice mill to produce a thick paste. Alternatively, pound the ingredients in a mortar with a pestle.

2 Heat the oil in a wok, add the paste and turmeric, and cook over a gentle heat, stirring frequently, for 3 minutes. Stir in the water and simmer gently for 3 minutes.

3 Stir in the coconut milk, lime juice, sugar and salt to taste. Simmer for a further 3 minutes. Add the prawns and stir-fry for 4–5 minutes, or until they turn pink and are cooked.

4 Season the curry to taste, then transfer it to a warmed serving dish. Garnish with spring onions and coconut, and serve immediately.

■ Coconut milk is available canned or dried or it can be made by dissolving creamed coconut in hot water. To make coconut milk from fresh or desiccated coconut, soak grated coconut in boiling water to cover for 30 minutes; drain well and squeeze out the 'milk.'

2 tablespoons groundnut oil

1 teaspoon turmeric

150 ml (¼ pint) water

150 ml (¼ pint) coconut milk

juice of 1 lime

2 teaspoons soft brown sugar

16 uncooked king prawns, peeled and deveined

salt and pepper

Spice Paste:

2 fresh red chillies, deseeded and chopped

2 shallots, chopped

1 lemon grass stalk, chopped

2.5 cm (1 inch) piece of fresh root ginger, peeled and chopped

¼ teaspoon Thai shrimp paste

To Garnish:

4 spring onions, cut into thin strips

thin slices of fresh coconut or 1 tablespoon desiccated coconut

Serves 4

Preparation time: 10 minutes

Cooking time: 15 minutes

250 g (8 oz) rice sticks

2 tablespoons vegetable oil

125 g (4 oz) radishes, trimmed and thinly sliced

375 g (12 oz) uncooked tiger prawns, peeled and deveined

juice of 1 lemon

1 tablespoon caster sugar

2 teaspoons fish sauce (nam pla)

1 teaspoon chilli powder, or to taste

salt

To Garnish:

sprigs of Thai sweet basil

1 tablespoon chopped coriander

Serves 2–3
Preparation time: 10 minutes
Cooking time: 10 minutes

1 Cook or soak the rice sticks in boiling salted water according to the packet instructions.

2 Meanwhile, heat the oil in a wok. Add the radishes and stir-fry over high heat for 30 seconds. Add the prawns and stir-fry for 1–2 minutes or until they just turn pink. Add the lemon juice, sugar, fish sauce and the chilli powder and stir-fry briskly for a further 1–2 minutes.

3 Drain the rice sticks, add them to the prawn mixture and add salt to taste. Toss until evenly mixed. Serve immediately, garnished with Thai basil and chopped coriander.

prawns with thai noodles

stir-fried prawns

1 Wash the prawns, remove their heads, shell and legs, but keep the tails intact. Dry thoroughly on kitchen paper and set aside.

2 Heat the oil in a wok or large frying pan until it is smoking hot. Add the ginger and fry for 30 seconds to flavour the oil. Use a slotted spoon to remove and discard the ginger.

3 Mix 6 teaspoons of the cornflour with the salt, sherry and egg white. Toss the prawns in this mixture until well coated, then add them to the hot oil and stir-fry until they turn pink. Use a slotted spoon to remove the prawns from the wok; then set them aside.

4 Add the garlic, black beans, mangetout and water chestnuts to the oil remaining in the wok and stir-fry for 1–2 minutes, then replace the prawns. Mix the remaining cornflour to a smooth paste with the soy sauce and chicken stock, then stir into the prawn mixture. Cook, stirring, until thickened.

5 Add the sesame oil to the prawns and toss well. Serve immediately, garnished with spring onions and sprigs of coriander, if using.

500 g (1 lb) uncooked large prawns in shells

4 tablespoons vegetable oil

3 slices of fresh ginger root, peeled

7 teaspoons cornflour

1 teaspoon salt

1 tablespoon dry sherry

1 egg white

2 garlic cloves, crushed

2 teaspoons black beans, soaked for 1 hour and drained

250 g (8 oz) mangetout, halved

6 water chestnuts, thinly sliced

½ tablespoon soy sauce

2 tablespoons chicken stock

1 tablespoon sesame oil

To Garnish: (optional)

shredded spring onions

sprigs of coriander

Serves 3–4
Preparation time: 10 minutes
Cooking time: 8–10 minutes

ginger fish steaks

1 Cut the fish steak into bite-sized pieces. Then mix together the salt, wine or sherry and 1 tablespoon of the cornflour, and marinate the fish in this mixture for about 30 minutes.

2 Dip the marinated fish pieces in the egg white, then in the remaining cornflour. Heat the oil in a wok or frying pan until hot, then fry the fish until golden, stirring occasionally.

3 Add the ginger, soy sauce, sugar and stock or water. Cook for about 3–4 minutes, or until the liquid has evaporated. Serve hot, garnished with the shredded spring onion.

■ Coating the fish in egg white and cornflour before adding to the wok or pan helps prevent the fish from breaking up during stir-frying.

500 g (1 lb) fish steak, such as cod, halibut or hake

½ teaspoon salt

2 tablespoons Chinese wine or dry sherry

4 tablespoons cornflour

1 egg white, lightly beaten

3 tablespoons sunflower oil

1 slice of fresh root ginger, peeled and finely chopped

2 tablespoons light soy sauce

2 teaspoons sugar

125 ml (4 fl oz) chicken stock or water

shredded spring onion, to garnish

Serves 4

Preparation time: 15 minutes, plus marinating

Cooking time: 15–20 minutes

scallop & prawn stir-fry with mixed vegetables

1 Cut each scallop into 3–4 pieces and place in a bowl. Leave the prawns whole if small, otherwise cut each into 2–3 pieces; add to the scallops. Add the egg white and about half the cornflour, then mix well.

2 Heat the oil for deep-frying in a wok or saucepan to 180–190°C (350–375°F) or until a day-old cube of bread browns in 30 seconds. Deep-fry the scallops and prawns for 1 minute, stirring them all the time with chop-sticks to keep the pieces separate. Use a slotted spoon to remove the scallops and prawns out of the oil and drain them on kitchen paper.

3 Pour off all but 2 tablespoons oil from the wok. Increase the heat to high and add the ginger and spring onions. Add the celery, pepper and carrots, and stir-fry for about 1 minute, then replace the scallops and prawns. Stir in the wine or sherry, soy sauce, chilli bean paste (if using) and season to taste with salt.

4 Mix the remaining cornflour to a smooth paste with a little water, then pour this into the wok and cook, stirring, until the sauce boils and thickens. Sprinkle the sesame seed oil over the mixture and serve immediately.

4–6 fresh scallops

125–175 g (4–6 oz) uncooked prawns, peeled and deveined

1 egg white

1 tablespoon cornflour

vegetable oil, for deep-frying

2 slices of fresh root ginger, peeled and finely shredded

2–3 spring onions, finely shredded

3 celery sticks, sliced

1 red pepper, cored, deseeded and diced

1–2 carrots, sliced

2 tablespoons Chinese wine or dry sherry

1 tablespoon light soy sauce

2 teaspoons chilli bean paste (optional)

1 teaspoon sesame oil

salt

Serves 4–6

Preparation time: 20–25 minutes

Cooking time: 6–8 minutes

mixed seafood with rice noodles & ginger

1 Soak the mushrooms in warm water for 15–20 minutes. Drain and squeeze the mushrooms, then discard the hard stalks and thinly slice the caps.

2 Cook or soak the rice noodles according to packet instructions, until they are just tender. Drain and rinse in cold water, then set aside.

3 Heat the oil in a wok or a large frying pan. Add the spring onions, garlic and ginger and stir-fry briskly for 30 seconds. Stir in the mushrooms, prawns and squid (if using), then cook for 2 minutes.

4 Add the clams, wine or sherry, soy sauce and season to taste with salt. Carefully stir in the noodles and heat through, then transfer the mixture into a warmed dish and serve immediately.

4 dried shiitake mushrooms

500 g (1 lb) rice noodles

2 tablespoons vegetable oil

4 spring onions, chopped

2 garlic cloves, sliced

1 piece of fresh root ginger, peeled and finely chopped

50 g (2 oz) cooked, peeled prawns, thawed if frozen

125 g (4 oz) squid rings (optional)

250 g (8 oz) can clams, drained

2 tablespoons Chinese wine or dry sherry

1 tablespoon soy sauce

salt

Serves 4–6

Preparation time: 10 minutes, plus soaking

Cooking time: about 10 minutes

2 tablespoons cornflour

2 tablespoons Chinese wine or dry sherry

1 tablespoon chicken stock or water

meat from 1 crab, about 875 g (1¾ lb) in weight

3 tablespoons sunflower oil

4 slices of fresh root ginger, peeled and finely chopped

4 spring onions, finely chopped

1 teaspoon salt

1 teaspoon light soy sauce

2 teaspoons sugar

1 Mix the cornflour to a smooth paste with half the wine or sherry and the stock or water. Add the crab and stir, taking care not to break it up too much. Leave to marinate for about 10 minutes.

2 Heat the oil in a wok or frying pan. Add the crab and stir-fry for 1 minute. Add the ginger, spring onions, salt, soy sauce, sugar and remaining wine or sherry. Cook for about 5 minutes, stirring constantly. Add a little water if the mixture becomes very dry. Serve immediately.

Serves 4

Preparation time: 25–30 minutes, plus marinating

Cooking time: 6 minutes

stir-fried crab with ginger & spring onions

■ Fresh crabs are a favourite ingredient in Chinese cooking. Most fishmongers sell prepared crab meat on the shell – buy 2 if they are small.

baby squid stir-fried with fresh herbs

1 To prepare the squid, hold the head and tentacles in one hand and pull away the body with the other. Pull the innards and the hard 'pen' away from the body and discard. Cut the tentacles from the head: reserve the tentacles and discard the head.

2 Sprinkle some salt on your fingers and rub the thin mottled skin from the body and tentacles. Rinse well and pat dry. Cut the flesh into slices. Season with salt and pepper.

3 Heat the oil in a wok over a gentle heat. Add the garlic and cook until browned. Remove with a slotted spoon and discard.

4 Increase the heat. When the oil is hot, add the squid and cook briskly for 1 minute, stirring to prevent the pieces sticking together. Add the coriander, parsley and lemon juice, and stir-fry for 30 seconds.

5 Transfer to a warmed serving dish. Garnish, if liked, with slices of lemon or lime, and tiny sprigs of coriander or parsley and serve.

1 kg (2 lb) baby squid
4 tablespoons sunflower oil
3–4 garlic cloves, sliced
2 tablespoons chopped coriander
1 tablespoon chopped flat leaf parsley
juice of ½ lemon
salt and pepper

To Garnish: (optional)
slices of lemon or lime
tiny sprigs of coriander or parsley

Serves 4
Preparation time: about 10 minutes
Cooking time: 2–4 minutes

■ Baby squid is the best to use for stir-frying, as its flesh is delicate and very tender. It must be cooked quickly or it becomes tough. It is ideal for stir-fried dishes such as this.

stir-fried fish with bacon & vegetables

1 Place the fish in a dish, sprinkle with the salt and leave to stand for 15 minutes. Drain, if necessary, and pat dry on kitchen paper.

2 Heat the oil in a wok or large frying pan over a moderate heat. Add the fish and bacon and stir-fry for 3 minutes.

3 Add the peas, sweetcorn, stock or water, wine or sherry, soy sauce and sugar. Bring to the boil. Blend the cornflour to a thin paste with a little water and add to the sauce, stirring continuously, then cook for 1 minute.

4 Transfer to a warmed dish and garnish with lemon slices, if using, and spring onion, and serve.

500 g (1 lb) skinless cod fillet, cut into wide strips

1 teaspoon salt

1 tablespoon oil

2 rashers of rindless back bacon, cut into fine strips

50 g (2 oz) peas, cooked

50 g (2 oz) sweetcorn, cooked

6 tablespoons chicken stock or water

2 tablespoons Chinese wine or dry sherry

2 teaspoons light soy sauce

1 teaspoon sugar

1 teaspoon cornflour

To Garnish:

lemon slices (optional)

finely shredded spring onion

Serves 4
Preparation time: 5 minutes, plus standing
Cooking time: 5–7 minutes

scrambled eggs with prawns & bean sprouts

1 Beat the eggs with the soy sauce. Heat the oil in a wok or a large frying pan over a high heat.

2 Add the onions, garlic and bean sprouts and stir-fry for 1 minute. Mix in the eggs and prawns. Cook, stirring constantly, until the eggs start to scramble. Serve hot, garnished with spring onion, if using.

8 eggs

3 tablespoons soy sauce

4 tablespoons oil

2 medium onions, thinly sliced

1 garlic clove, finely chopped

150 g (5 oz) bean sprouts

125 g (4 oz) shelled prawns

chopped spring onion, to garnish

Serves 4
Preparation time: 10 minutes
Cooking time: 5–6 minutes

■ Bean sprouts are the sprouts of small green mung beans. Although they are available in cans, it is best to use them as fresh as possible. You can grow your own beansprouts by putting some mung beans in a jam jar, covering it with muslin and securing it with an elastic band. Rinse the beans every day until the sprouts are long enough.

sweet & sour swordfish

1 Mix all the ingredients for the marinade in a shallow dish. Add the swordfish and turn the pieces to coat them evenly. Cover and leave to marinate for about 30 minutes, turning the fish occasionally.

2 Heat the wok until hot. Add 2 tablespoons of the oil and heat until hot. Use a slotted spoon to remove the swordfish strips from the marinade, draining off as much liquid as possible, and add them to the pan. Reserve the marinade. Stir-fry the swordfish for 3–5 minutes, or until tender. Remove the wok from the heat and use a slotted spoon to transfer the swordfish to a plate. Set aside.

3 Mix the cornflour to a paste with a little of the fish stock, then stir in the reserved marinade and the remaining stock. Set aside.

4 Return the wok to a moderate heat. Add the remaining oil and heat until hot. Stir-fry the pepper strips for 5 minutes. Stir the cornflour mixture, then pour it into the wok and bring to the boil, stirring continuously.

5 Return the swordfish and its juices to the wok. Increase the heat and stir-fry for 1–2 minutes or until all the ingredients are combined and piping hot. Serve immediately.

500 g (1 lb) swordfish fillet, cut into chunky strips

3 tablespoons vegetable oil

1 tablespoon cornflour

125 ml (4 fl oz) cold fish stock

1 green pepper, cored, deseeded and cut into thin strips

1 red pepper, cored, deseeded and cut into thin strips

Marinade:

3 tablespoons soy sauce

2 tablespoons rice wine or dry sherry

1 tablespoon red or white wine vinegar

1 tablespoon soft brown sugar

Serves 4

Preparation time: 15 minutes, plus marinating

Cooking time: 9–12 minutes

tangy fried chicken livers with broccoli ●

chicken with green peppers ●

ginger chicken with honey ●

chicken chop suey ●

fried eight-piece chicken ●

stir-fried sesame chicken ●

chicken with shrimp sauce ●

chicken with pineapple ●

lemon chicken ●

malaysian orange chicken ●

ginger chicken with baby mushrooms ●

bang bang chicken ●

stir-fried duck with bamboo shoots & almonds ●

oriental duckling ●

sesame marinated turkey ●

more than
chicken

58

tangy fried chicken livers with broccoli

1 Heat the oil and butter in a wok or large frying pan. Stir-fry the garlic for 1 minute. Add the mushrooms and chicken livers and cook for 5 minutes, stirring occasionally, until the chicken livers are browned.

2 Add the broccoli, orange rind and juice, sherry and ground ginger. Season the mixture with a little salt and plenty of pepper. Bring to the boil, reduce the heat, cover and simmer for 5–6 minutes, or until the broccoli is just tender but still crisp.

3 Adjust the seasoning to taste and transfer to a serving dish. Garnish with parsley and serve immediately.

2 tablespoons sesame oil

25 g (1 oz) butter

2 garlic cloves, crushed

250 g (8 oz) mushrooms, thinly sliced

500 g (1 lb) chicken livers, roughly chopped

125 g (4 oz) broccoli, roughly chopped

1 tablespoon grated orange rind

4 tablespoons orange juice

2 tablespoons dry sherry

pinch of ground ginger

salt and pepper

2 tablespoons chopped parsley, to garnish

Serves 4	
Preparation time: 20 minutes	
Cooking time: 11–12 minutes	

chicken with green peppers

1 Season the chicken with ½ teaspoon of the salt, then mix it with the egg white and add 2 teaspoons of the cornflour. Mix well. Blend the remaining cornflour to a smooth paste with a little water.

2 Heat the oil in a wok or a large frying pan. Stir-fry the chicken over a moderate heat until they turn white, then remove them from the wok with a slotted spoon and set aside.

3 Increase the heat to high. When the oil is very hot, add the spring onion and ginger. Add the peppers and stir-fry for 30 seconds, then replace the chicken and add the remaining salt and the rice wine or sherry. Stir-fry for 1 minute.

4 Pour in the cornflour, stirring, and cook briefly until the liquid has thickened. Serve at once, garnished with sesame seeds, spring onion strips, lime wedges and chilli slices.

2 boneless, skinless chicken breasts, cut into thin strips

1½ teaspoons salt

1 egg white, lightly beaten

3 teaspoons cornflour

4 tablespoons vegetable oil

1 spring onion, finely chopped

2 slices of fresh root ginger, peeled and finely chopped

250 g (8 oz) green peppers, cored, deseeded and cut into short fine strips

2 tablespoons rice wine or dry sherry

To Garnish:

1 teaspoon sesame seeds

spring onion strips

lime wedges

red chilli slices

Serves 4

Preparation time: 10–15 minutes

Cooking time: 10 minutes

1 Place the ginger in a small bowl. Add a little cold water, mix well, then drain and squeeze the ginger until it is dry.

2 Heat the oil in a wok. Stir-fry the chopped chicken and livers over a moderate heat for 5 minutes. Use a slotted spoon to remove the chicken mixture from the wok and set aside.

3 Add the onion and fry gently until soft, then add the garlic and the drained black fungus, and stir-fry for 1 minute. Return the chicken mixture to the wok.

4 Stir the soy sauce and honey in a bowl until blended, then pour this over the chicken and stir well. Add the ginger and stir-fry for 2–3 minutes. Add the spring onions and serve, garnished with strips of chilli and accompanied by rice sticks, if liked.

50 g (2 oz) fresh root ginger, peeled and finely chopped

2 tablespoons vegetable oil

3 boneless, skinless chicken breasts, chopped

3 chicken livers, chopped

1 onion, finely sliced

3 garlic cloves, crushed

2 tablespoons dried black fungus (cloud's ears), soaked in hot water for 20 minutes and drained

1 tablespoon soy sauce

1 tablespoon honey

5 spring onions, chopped

1 red chilli, deseeded and cut into fine strips, to garnish

rice sticks, to serve (optional)

Serves 4

Preparation time: 15 minutes, plus soaking

Cooking time: 10–15 minutes

ginger chicken with honey

■ This dish tastes even better if cooked the day before, cooled and chilled, then thoroughly reheated before being served.

chicken chop suey

1 Heat 1 tablespoon of the oil, add the spring onions and ginger, and stir-fry for 1 minute.

2 Add the garlic and chicken, and stir-fry for 2 minutes. Lower the heat, and add the tomato purée, the wine or sherry, soy sauce, sugar and 5 tablespoons of the water.

3 Heat through gently, then transfer to a warmed serving dish. Heat two teaspoons of the oil in the pan, add the bean sprouts and remaining water, and stir-fry for 3 minutes.

4 Add to the serving dish and keep warm. Wipe out the pan and heat the remaining oil. Pour in the beaten eggs and cook gently until set and crisp. Cut into thin strips and place on top of the bean sprout mixture and serve immediately.

2 tablespoons oil

5 spring onions, chopped

2.5 cm (1 inch) piece fresh root ginger, peeled and chopped

2 garlic cloves, crushed

175 g (6 oz) chicken breast, skinned and cut into thin strips

1 tablespoon tomato purée

2 tablespoons Chinese wine or dry sherry

2 tablespoons soy sauce

1 teaspoon sugar

8 tablespoons water

300 g (10 oz) bean sprouts

3 eggs, beaten with 2 tablespoons water

Serves 4

Preparation time: 8 minutes

Cooking time: 8–10 minutes

■ The term Chop Suey comes from the Chinese word 'zasui' which means 'mixed bits.' Small portions of meat, fish and vegetables can be added – a great way to use up left-overs.

fried eight-piece chicken

1 Carefully cut off the legs, wings and breasts from the chicken. Then cut each breast in half.

2 In a bowl large enough to hold all the chicken, mix the spring onions and ginger with 1 tablespoon of the sherry, 1 teaspoon of the sugar and 1 tablespoon of the soy sauce. Turn the chicken in this marinade until they are well coated. Cover and leave to marinate for about 5 minutes.

3 Remove the chicken from the marinade, draining each piece well, and dust with cornflour. Reserve any leftover marinade.

4 Heat the lard in a wok or large frying pan. Fry the chicken over moderate heat until golden brown and cooked through. Pour off the excess lard, leaving the chicken in the wok.

5 Add the remaining sherry, sugar, soy sauce and leftover marinade. Bring to the boil, stirring. Stir in the sesame oil and serve immediately, garnished with chives.

1.25 kg (2½ lb) spring chicken, rinsed and dried

2–3 spring onions, finely chopped

2–3 slices of fresh root ginger, peeled and finely chopped

2 tablespoons dry sherry

1 tablespoon sugar

3 tablespoons soy sauce

3 tablespoons cornflour

125 g (4 oz) lard or butter

1 teaspoon sesame oil

snipped chives, to garnish

Serves 4
Preparation time: 20 minutes
Cooking time: 15 minutes

1 Place the chicken in a bowl, sprinkle with the cornflour and toss until all the pieces are evenly coated. Heat the oil in a wok and stir-fry the chicken over a high heat for 45 seconds. Use a slotted spoon to remove the chicken from the wok and set aside.

2 Add the green pepper and stir-fry over moderate heat for 1 minute. Stir in 1 tablespoon of the soy sauce, then remove the green pepper with a slotted spoon and set aside.

3 Add the remaining soy sauce, the sesame seed paste, sesame oil, stock or water, chilli sauce and sherry. Cook, stirring, for 1 minute, then replace the chicken and stir over a high heat for about 45 seconds. Stir in the reserved green pepper and cook for a further 30 seconds or until the pepper is just tender.

4 Transfer the chicken mixture to a serving dish and garnish with the sesame seeds. Serve immediately.

500 g (1 lb) boneless, skinless chicken breasts, cut into 2.5 cm (1 inch) cubes

1½ teaspoons cornflour

4 tablespoons vegetable oil

1 green pepper, cored, deseeded and cut into 2.5 cm (1 inch) pieces

2½ tablespoons soy sauce

2½ tablespoons sesame seed paste

1 tablespoon sesame oil

1 tablespoon chicken stock or water

1 teaspoon chilli sauce

1 tablespoon dry sherry

sesame seeds, to garnish

Serves 3–4
Preparation time: 10 minutes
Cooking time: 7–8 minutes

stir-fried sesame chicken

chicken with shrimp sauce

1 Cut the chicken joints into small portions, each about 4 cm (1½ inch) long. Purée the onion, garlic, ginger and chillies with the water in a food processor or blender.

2 Heat the oil in a wok and fry the onion purée for 3 4 minutes. Add the turmeric, pepper, shrimp paste and laos powder, if using, and cook briskly for 1 minute. Add the lemon rind, fish sauce, salt and chicken pieces and stir-fry until the chicken starts to brown.

3 Pour in the coconut milk, then stir in the sugar and bring to the boil. Simmer, covered, for 30 minutes or until the chicken is cooked through and tender. Stir in the lemon juice and serve immediately.

1.5 kg (3 lb) chicken joints

1 onion, quartered

4 garlic cloves, peeled

2.5 cm (1 inch) piece of fresh root ginger, peeled and chopped

3 fresh red chillies, deseeded and quartered

1 tablespoon water

3 tablespoons sunflower oil

1 teaspoon turmeric

1 teaspoon pepper

½ teaspoon dried shrimp paste

½ teaspoon laos powder (optional)

2 strips of lemon rind

2 teaspoons fish sauce (nam pla)

1½ teaspoons salt

300 ml (½ pint) coconut milk

1 tablespoon sugar

2 tablespoons lemon juice

Serves 4
Preparation time: 30 minutes
Cooking time: about 40 minutes

■ Thigh portions are ideal for this recipe; use a meat cleaver to chop each into 2 or 3 smaller portions.

chicken with pineapple

1 Cut the chicken into bite-sized pieces. Using a fork, whisk the egg white with a little salt and pepper until frothy. Sift in the cornflour and whisk until well mixed, then add the chicken and stir until coated.

2 Heat the oil in a wok until very hot but not smoking. Stir-fry about a quarter of the chicken for 30–60 seconds, until the chicken turns white. Use a slotted spoon to remove the chicken and drain on kitchen paper. Repeat with the remaining chicken. Carefully pour off all but about 1 tablespoon of the hot oil from the wok.

3 Return the wok to a low heat and make the sauce: stir-fry the onion, carrot and ginger for 3 minutes or until softened but not browned. Pour in the stock or water, orange and lemon juices and increase the heat. Bring to the boil, stirring, then stir in the soy sauce, vinegar and 1 teaspoon of sugar.

4 Put the chicken in the sauce and cook over a moderate to high heat, stirring occasionally, for about 3 minutes. Add the pineapple and juice and cook for 1 minute.

5 Blend the cornflour to a smooth paste with a little cold water. Add to the chicken and simmer, stirring, for 2 minutes, until thickened. Season to taste, adding more sugar if liked. Serve hot, garnished with carrot or orange rind and spring onion strips.

2 boneless, skinless chicken breasts, about 250–300 g (8–10 oz) total weight

1 egg white

2 teaspoons cornflour

75 ml (3 fl oz) groundnut oil

125 g (4 oz) prepared pineapple, cut into bite-sized pieces, with juice reserved

salt and pepper

Sauce:

1 small onion, cut into chunks

1 carrot, cut into short fine strips

2.5 cm (1 inch) piece of fresh root ginger, peeled and cut into fine strips

150 ml (¼ pint) cold chicken stock or water

200 ml (7 fl oz) orange juice

2 tablespoons lemon juice

1 tablespoon light soy sauce

1 tablespoon white wine vinegar

1–2 teaspoons sugar, to taste

2 teaspoons cornflour

To Garnish:

fine strips of carrot or orange rind

fine strips of spring onion

Serves 2–4

Preparation time: 15 minutes

Cooking time: about 20 minutes

lemon chicken

1 First prepare the sauce. Mix the cornflour to a thin paste with the stock or water, then add the remaining sauce ingredients, stirring well.

2 In a shallow dish, lightly beat the egg white with the cornflour and salt. Add the strips of chicken and turn them to coat them with the egg white mixture. Set aside.

3 Heat the oil in a wok until hot but not smoking. Use a fork to add the strips of chicken individually into the hot oil. Stir-fry for 3–4 minutes or until golden – do this in batches as the pieces will not cook evenly if too many are added at once. Use a slotted spoon to remove the chicken and drain the pieces on kitchen paper. Keep hot.

4 Pour off all but 1 tablespoon oil from the wok. Stir-fry the spring onions and garlic over a moderate heat for 30 seconds. Stir the sauce and pour it into the wok, stirring continuously. Increase the heat to high and bring to the boil, stirring.

5 Return the chicken to the wok and stir-fry for 1–2 minutes or until evenly coated in the sauce. Garnish with lemon slices and serve.

1 egg white

2 teaspoons cornflour

pinch of salt

2 boneless, skinless chicken breasts, about 300 g (10 oz) total weight, cut across the grain into thin strips

300 ml (½ pint) vegetable oil

½ bunch of spring onions, shredded

1 garlic clove, crushed

lemon slices, to garnish

Sauce:

2 teaspoons cornflour

4 tablespoons cold chicken stock or water

finely grated rind of ½ lemon

2 tablespoons lemon juice

1 tablespoon soy sauce

2 teaspoons rice wine or dry sherry

2 teaspoons caster sugar

Serves 2
Preparation time: 15 minutes
Cooking time: 4–6 minutes

1 Using a fork, lightly whisk the egg whites with the cornflour and a pinch of salt in a shallow dish. Add the chicken and turn the strips to coat them evenly. Mix all the ingredients for the sauce and set aside.

2 Heat the oil in a wok until hot but not smoking. Use a fork to add the strips of chicken individually into the hot oil. Fry for 3–4 minutes or until golden – you will have to do this in batches as the pieces will not cook evenly if too many are added at once. Use a slotted spoon to remove the chicken and drain the pieces on kitchen paper. Keep hot.

3 Pour off almost all the oil from the wok. Add the spring onions and stir-fry briskly over a moderate heat for 30 seconds. Pour in the sauce and bring to the boil, stirring, then add the peas and salt and pepper to taste. Simmer, stirring frequently, for about 5 minutes or until the peas are cooked.

4 Replace the chicken in the wok and toss for 1–2 minutes or until all the ingredients are well combined and piping hot. Serve garnished with orange slices and flat leaf parsley.

malaysian orange chicken

2 egg whites

2 tablespoons cornflour

4 boneless, skinless chicken breasts, about 625 g (1¼ lb) total weight, cut across the grain into thin strips

about 300 ml (½ pint) vegetable oil

1 bunch of spring onions, thinly sliced diagonally

125 g (4 oz) fresh or frozen peas

salt and pepper

Sauce:

175 ml (6 fl oz) fresh orange juice

3–4 tablespoons concentrated orange squash, or to taste

2 tablespoons soy sauce

1 tablespoon cider vinegar

1 teaspoon soft brown sugar

To Garnish:

orange slices

sprigs of flat leaf parsley

Serves 3–4

Preparation time: 15minutes

Cooking time: 10–15 minutes

ginger chicken
with baby mushrooms

1 Place the chicken pieces in a bowl, sprinkle with the sugar and leave to stand for 20–30 minutes. Season with salt and pepper. Blend the cornflour to a smooth paste with 3 tablespoons of water and set aside.

2 Heat the oil in a wok and fry the ginger for 1 minute. Add the chicken and stir-fry for 3 minutes.

3 Pour in the remaining water and stir in the mushrooms. Bring to the boil, then reduce the heat. Cover and simmer for 5 minutes or until the chicken is tender.

4 Add the brandy, soy sauce and season to taste. Stir the cornflour mixture and pour it into the chicken, stirring. Bring to the boil, stirring, and cook for about 30–60 seconds or until the sauce is thickened; then serve hot.

750 g (1½ lb) boneless, skinless chicken breasts, cut into finger-sized pieces

1 teaspoon sugar

2 teaspoons cornflour

4 tablespoons sesame oil

10 cm (4 inch) piece of fresh root ginger, peeled and finely sliced

75–100 ml (3–3½ fl oz), plus 3 tablespoons, water

125 g (4 oz) button mushrooms

2 tablespoons brandy

1 teaspoon light soy sauce

salt and pepper

Serves 4

Preparation time: 10 minutes, plus standing

Cooking time: 10–15 minutes

bang bang chicken

1. Place the chicken breasts between 2 sheets of greaseproof paper and bang hard with a rolling pin to flatten and tenderize them. Cut the chicken into thin strips across the grain, then place in a shallow dish. Mix 2 tablespoons of the soy sauce with the sesame oil and ginger. Pour over the chicken and turn to coat. Cover and leave to marinate for 20 minutes.

2. Meanwhile, heat the wok until hot. Dry-fry the sesame seeds over a gentle heat for 1–2 minutes or until toasted, tossing so they do not burn. Remove the wok from the heat and tip the seeds on to a plate.

3. Return the wok to a moderate heat with 2 tablespoons of the vegetable oil. Add the carrots and chilli and stir-fry for 2–3 minutes. Remove with a slotted spoon and place in a bowl. Add the bean sprouts to the wok and stir-fry for 1 minute, then tip the bean sprouts into a bowl. Add the cucumber strips and toss well.

4. Heat the remaining oil in the wok. Add the chicken, increase the heat and stir-fry for 4–5 minutes. Transfer the chicken to a separate bowl. Add the remaining soy sauce, the rice wine or sherry, honey and stock to the wok. Bring to the boil, stirring, then simmer briefly, stirring constantly, until reduced slightly. Pour half of the sauce over the vegetables and half over the chicken. Stir to mix, then cover and leave to cool, stirring occasionally.

5. Arrange the mixtures on plates, drizzle over any remaining sauce and sprinkle with the sesame seeds. Garnish with parsley and serve.

4 chicken breasts, boned and skinned

6 tablespoons soy sauce

2 tablespoons sesame oil

2.5 cm (1 inch) piece of fresh root ginger, peeled and finely chopped

2 tablespoons sesame seeds

4 tablespoons vegetable oil

4 carrots, cut into julienne strips

1 fresh green or red chilli, deseeded and chopped

125 g (4 oz) bean sprouts

½ cucumber, cut into julienne strips

3 tablespoons rice wine or dry sherry

2 tablespoons clear honey

150 ml (¼ pint) chicken stock

flat leaf parsley, to garnish

Serves 4

Preparation time: about 30 minutes, plus cooling

Cooking time: about 15 minutes

stir-fried duck with bamboo shoots & almonds

1 Place the duck in a large bowl with the ginger and garlic. Add 1 tablespoon of the oil, mix well and leave to marinate for 30 minutes.

2 Soak the mushrooms in warm water for 15 minutes, then drain and squeeze them dry. Discard the stalks and slice the mushroom caps.

3 Heat the remaining oil in a wok or large frying pan and stir-fry the spring onions for 30 seconds. Add the duck and stir-fry for 2 minutes. Add the mushrooms, bamboo shoots, soy sauce and wine or sherry, and cook for 2 minutes.

4 Blend the cornflour to a smooth paste with the water and stir into the duck mixture. Cook for 1 minute, stirring, until thickened. Stir in the almonds and serve immediately.

500 g (1 lb) boneless, skinless duck breast, cut into small chunks

2 slices of fresh root ginger, peeled and shredded

1 garlic clove, crushed

3 tablespoons sesame oil

3–4 dried shiitake mushrooms

4 spring onions, sliced

125 g (4 oz) can bamboo shoots, drained and sliced

3 tablespoons soy sauce

2 tablespoons Chinese wine or dry sherry

2 teaspoons cornflour

1 tablespoon water

25 g (1 oz) flaked almonds, toasted

Serves 4–6

Preparation time: 15 minutes, plus marinating and soaking

Cooking time: 6–7 minutes

oriental duckling

1 Check the weight of the duckling and calculate the cooking time at 30 minutes per 500 g (1 lb). Prick the duckling all over with a fork and place in a roasting tin. Sprinkle with salt and roast in a preheated oven, 190°C (375°F), Gas Mark 5, for the calculated cooking time, until golden brown and cooked through. Leave to cool, then strip the flesh and skin from the carcass and cut into thin strips.

2 Heat 2 tablespoons of the oil in a wok or large frying pan. Add the onion, mushrooms, garlic and peppers and stir-fry for 4 minutes. Use a slotted spoon to transfer the mixture to a plate and keep warm.

3 Heat the remaining oil in the wok or pan. Stir-fry the meat and skin with the bean sprouts for 3 minutes. Remove from the wok; keep warm.

4 Blend the cornflour to a smooth paste with the soy sauce and sherry, then stir in the stock. Pour this sauce into the wok and bring to the boil, stirring. Reduce the heat and simmer for 2 minutes.

5 Stir in the almonds and add the cooked ingredients. Taste and adjust the seasoning. Heat through for 3 minutes, then serve with boiled rice and crisp-fried noodles, if liked.

2 kg (4 lb) oven-ready duckling

5 tablespoons corn oil

1 large onion, thinly sliced

125 g (4 oz) button mushrooms, thickly sliced

1 garlic clove, crushed

1 small red pepper, cored, deseeded and cut into thin strips

1 small green pepper, cored, deseeded and cut into thin strips

250 g (8 oz) bean sprouts

1 tablespoon cornflour

1 tablespoon soy sauce

2–3 teaspoons dry sherry

300 ml (½ pint) chicken stock

125 g (4 oz) blanched almonds, toasted

salt and pepper

Serves 4
Preparation time: 30 minutes
Cooking time: 2 hours 12 minutes

sesame marinated turkey

1 Mix all the marinade ingredients in a bowl. Add the turkey cubes and turn them in the marinade until they are thoroughly coated. Cover and leave in a cool place for 30 minutes.

2 Meanwhile, heat the oil in a wok or large frying pan. Stir-fry the cashew nuts until golden brown. Use a slotted spoon to remove the nuts from the pan and drain on kitchen paper, then set aside and keep warm.

3 Add the turkey and its marinade and stir-fry for 2 minutes. Add the mushrooms and cook for 1 minute. Transfer the mixture to warmed plates, sprinkle with the cashews, spring onions and red pepper and serve.

500 g (1 lb) boneless, skinless turkey breast, cut into small cubes

1 tablespoon vegetable oil

125 g (4 oz) unsalted cashew nuts

75 g (3 oz) button or shiitake mushrooms, halved

Sesame Marinade:

3 spring onions, chopped

3 tablespoons soy sauce

2 tablespoons chilli oil

2 tablespoons sesame oil

1 tablespoon sesame seed paste

1 teaspoon ground Szechuan pepper

To Serve:

1–2 spring onions, finely shredded

1 red pepper, cored, deseeded and finely shredded

Serves 4
Preparation time: 10 minutes, plus marinating
Cooking time: 6–7 minutes

lamb with spicy hot sauce •
lamb & courgette fritters •
spring lamb stir-fried with garlic •
fried pork with baby corn & mangetout •
sweet & sour pork •
spicy pork meatballs •
stir-fried pork with aubergine •
pork with bean sprouts •
szechuan dry-fried shredded beef •
beef with broccoli •
stir-fried beef with plum sauce & mushrooms •
fried beef with french beans •
stir-fried liver & spinach •
stir-fried beef in hot chilli sauce •

for meat's sake

lamb with spicy hot sauce

1 First prepare the ingredients for the sauce. Blend the cornflour to a thin paste with the cold water, then stir in the chilli sauce, vinegar, sugar and five-spice powder.

2 Heat 2 tablespoons of the oil in a wok. Stir-fry the lamb over a high heat for 3–4 minutes or until browned on all sides. Tip the lamb and its juices into a bowl.

3 Reduce the heat to moderate. Add the remaining oil and heat until hot, then stir-fry the spring onions and garlic for 30 seconds. Remove with a slotted spoon.

4 Stir the sauce to combine the ingredients, then pour it into the wok and increase the heat to high. Bring to the boil, stirring, and cook briefly until the sauce thickens.

5 Add the lamb and its juices, and the spring onion mixture. Toss the ingredients in the sauce until piping hot. Garnish with a few small chillies if using and serve immediately, with noodles.

3 tablespoons groundnut oil

500 g (1 lb) lamb neck fillet, trimmed and cut across the grain into thin strips

4 spring onions, sliced diagonally

2 garlic cloves, crushed

6–8 small chillies, to garnish (optional)

bean thread noodles, to serve

Sauce:

2 teaspoons cornflour

4 tablespoons cold water

2 tablespoons hot chilli sauce

1 tablespoon rice wine vinegar, white wine vinegar or cider vinegar

2 teaspoons dark soft brown sugar

½ teaspoon five-spice powder

Serves 3–4

Preparation time: 10 minutes

Cooking time: about 10 minutes

lamb & courgette fritters

1 Coat the courgette rounds in the seasoned flour. Put the sesame seeds in a wok or a large frying pan and dry-fry over a moderate heat for 1–2 minutes until toasted; remove from the pan and set aside.

2 Mix the minced lamb with the spring onion, garlic and toasted sesame seeds. Press this mixture on to one side of each courgette round, then coat the rounds in more flour.

3 Heat the oil in the wok to 180–190°C (350–375°F) or until a cube of day-old bread browns in 30 seconds. Gently dip the courgette rounds into the beaten eggs a few at a time, then fry in batches until golden brown, turning over once. Lift out of the oil with a slotted spoon, drain on kitchen paper and keep hot while frying the remainder. Garnish with parsley and serve warm.

2 large courgettes, sliced into 12 rounds

3–4 tablespoons plain flour, seasoned with salt and pepper

2 tablespoons sesame seeds

50 g (2 oz) minced lamb

1 spring onion, finely chopped

1 garlic clove, crushed

vegetable oil, for deep-frying

2 eggs, beaten

parsley sprigs, to garnish

Serves 4

Preparation time: 15 minutes

Cooking time: about 20 minutes

spring lamb stir-fried with garlic

1 In a bowl mix the wine or sherry with the soy sauces and sesame oil. Add the lamb and toss to evenly coat all the slices. Cover and leave to marinate for 15 minutes.

2 Drain the lamb, reserving the marinade. Heat the vegetable oil in a wok or large frying pan. Add the meat with 2 teaspoons of marinade and fry briskly for about 2 minutes or until the meat is well browned. Add a little extra marinade, if necessary, to prevent the meat from sticking.

3 Add the garlic, ginger, leek and spring onions and stir-fry for a further 3 minutes. Serve immediately.

2 tablespoons Chinese wine or dry sherry

2 tablespoons light soy sauce

1 tablespoon dark soy sauce

1 teaspoon sesame oil

375 g (12 oz) lamb fillet, thinly sliced across the grain

2 tablespoons vegetable oil

6 garlic cloves, thinly sliced

2.5 cm (1 inch) piece of fresh root ginger, peeled and chopped

1 leek, thinly sliced diagonally

4 spring onions, chopped

Serves 4

Preparation time: 5 minutes, plus marinating

Cooking time: 5–7 minutes

■ Meat is thinly sliced for stir-frying so that it's as tender as possible and cooks rapidly. It should be cut across the grain using a sharp knife or cleaver. Placing the meat in the freezer for about 1 hour before slicing makes it firm for easy cutting.

fried pork with baby corn & mangetout

1 Mix 1 teaspoon of the cornflour to a smooth paste with the wine or sherry and soy sauce. Add the pork and toss to coat all the slices with the cornflour paste.

2 Heat the oil in a wok or frying pan and stir-fry the pork until it is lightly browned.

3 Add the baby sweetcorn and salt, and stir-fry for 30 seconds. Add the mangetout and mushrooms, and stir-fry for 1 minute. Sprinkle the sugar over the pork mixture.

4 Mix the remaining cornflour with the water to make a thin paste and pour this into the wok, stirring continuously. Continue to cook briefly, stirring, until the sauce is thickened. Serve immediately.

1½ teaspoons cornflour

1 tablespoon Chinese wine or dry sherry

1 tablespoon light soy sauce

500 g (1 lb) pork fillet, very thinly sliced

1 tablespoon sunflower oil

500 g (1 lb) baby sweetcorn

1 teaspoon salt

50 g (2 oz) mangetout

475 g (15 oz) can straw mushrooms, drained

2 teaspoons sugar

2 teaspoons water

Serves 4
Preparation time: 5 minutes
Cooking time: 5–8 minutes

1 Cut the pork into small cubes and place them in a bowl. Sprinkle with the salt and brandy, then leave to marinate for 15 minutes. Add the beaten egg and cornflour and stir well.

2 Heat the oil in a wok to 180–190°C (350–375°F) or until a cube of day-old bread browns in 30 seconds. Meanwhile, coat the pork with flour, then fry for 3 minutes. Remove the wok from the heat, but leave the pork in the oil for 2 minutes. Use a slotted spoon to remove the pork from the oil.

3 Reheat the oil and re-fry the meat with the bamboo shoots for about 2 minutes. Remove and drain on kitchen paper. Carefully pour off all but 1 tablespoon of the oil. Add the spring onions and green pepper and stir-fry for 1 minute.

4 Mix the sauce ingredients with a little juice from the canned pineapple and stir into the wok. Bring to the boil and simmer briefly until thickened. Taste and add more juice if required. Add the pork, bamboo shoots and pineapple, mix lightly and serve hot.

250 g (8 oz) lean boneless pork

1 teaspoon salt

1½ tablespoons brandy

1 egg, beaten

1 tablespoon cornflour

vegetable oil, for deep-frying

3 tablespoons plain flour

125 g (4 oz) can bamboo shoots, drained and cut into small chunks

2 spring onions, cut into 2.5 cm (1 inch) lengths

1 green pepper, cored, deseeded and cut into small chunks

425 g (14 oz) can pineapple chunks in juice

Sauce:

3 tablespoons vinegar

3 tablespoons sugar

½ teaspoon salt

1 tablespoon tomato purée

1 tablespoon soy sauce

1 tablespoon cornflour

1 teaspoon sesame oil

Serves 3–4	
Preparation time: 15 minutes, plus marinating	
Cooking time: 15 minutes	

sweet & sour pork

spicy pork meatballs

1 Put the pork into a bowl. Drain the crab meat in a sieve and squeeze it to remove as much liquid as possible, then add to the pork. Add half of the ginger, garlic, chillies and coriander with 1 tablespoon of the soy sauce. Season with salt and pepper.

2 Mix the ingredients well, using your hands, and squeeze the mixture so that it binds together. With wet hands, form the mixture into about 24 balls. Coat the meatballs in the cornflour.

3 Heat the oil in a wok until very hot but not smoking. Cook the meatballs in batches for 2–3 minutes each, until golden and crisp all over. Remove with a slotted spoon and drain on kitchen paper.

4 Pour off all the oil from the wok and wipe it clean with kitchen paper. Return the meatballs to the wok and sprinkle with the remaining ginger, garlic and chilli. Pour in the hot stock and remaining soy sauce, sprinkle with the sugar and season to taste, then heat until simmering gently. Cover and cook gently for 15 minutes, turning the meatballs occasionally.

5 Add the Chinese leaves, stirring them into the liquid. Simmer for 5 minutes. Serve hot, sprinkled with the remaining coriander, the chilli strips and spring onions.

250 g (8 oz) minced pork

175 g (6 oz) can white crab meat in brine

5 cm (2 inch) piece of fresh root ginger, peeled and grated

2 garlic cloves, crushed

2 large fresh red chillies, deseeded and finely chopped

2 handfuls of coriander leaves, roughly chopped

3 tablespoons soy sauce

2 tablespoons cornflour

about 175 ml (6 fl oz) groundnut oil, for frying

600 ml (1 pint) hot chicken stock

1 teaspoon sugar

175–200 g (6–7 oz) Chinese leaves, shredded

salt and pepper

To Garnish:

1 large red chilli, deseeded and thinly sliced

4 spring onions, shredded

Serves 4–6
Preparation time: 30 minutes
Cooking time: 35–40 minutes

stir-fried pork with aubergine

1 In a bowl, mix the pork with the spring onions, ginger, garlic, soy sauce, wine or sherry and cornflour. Cover and leave to marinate for about 20 minutes.

2 Heat the oil for deep-frying to 180°C (350°F) or until a cube of day-old bread browns in 30 seconds. Reduce the heat, add the aubergine and deep-fry for about 1½ minutes. Remove from the pan with a slotted spoon and drain on kitchen paper.

3 Heat 1 tablespoon of the oil from deep-frying in a wok or frying pan, then stir-fry the pork for about 1 minute. Add the aubergine and chilli sauce and cook for about 1½ minutes.

4 Moisten the pork mixture with the stock or water and simmer until the liquid has almost completely evaporated. Garnish with chopped spring onions and serve hot, with plain boiled rice.

175 g (6 oz) lean boneless pork, shredded

2 spring onions, finely chopped

1 slice of fresh root ginger, peeled and finely chopped

1 garlic clove, finely chopped

1 tablespoon soy sauce

1 teaspoon Chinese wine or dry sherry

1½ teaspoons cornflour

vegetable oil, for deep-frying

250 g (8 oz) aubergine, cut into diamond-shaped chunks

1 tablespoon chilli sauce

3–4 tablespoons chicken stock or water

chopped spring onion, to garnish

Serves 3–4

Preparation time: 10 minutes, plus marinating

Cooking time: 10–15 minutes

pork with bean sprouts

1 Mix the cornflour to a smooth paste with the soy sauce, stock, sherry and vinegar.

2 Heat the oil in a wok. Add the onion and the garlic and fry for 30 seconds. Add the pork and bean sprouts, season to taste with salt and pepper and stir-fry the mixture for a further 1 minute.

3 Pour in the cornflour mixture, stirring, and stir-fry for a further 1½ minutes, until the juices boil and thicken. Serve immediately.

2 teaspoons cornflour

2 tablespoons soy sauce

4 tablespoons chicken stock

2 teaspoons dry sherry

2 tablespoons wine vinegar

5 tablespoons sunflower oil

2 tablespoons finely chopped onion

1 garlic clove, crushed

250 g (8 oz) lean pork fillet, cut into thin slices

125 g (4 oz) bean sprouts

salt and pepper

Serves 4
Preparation time: 10 minutes
Cooking time: 3 minutes

■ Thinly sliced beef can be used instead of pork and 125 g (4 oz) thinly sliced mushrooms can be added to either version, with an extra 1-2 teaspoons sherry.

szechuan dry-fried shredded beef

1 Heat a wok or large frying pan over a high heat for 1 minute. Add the sesame oil and reduce the heat to moderate. Add the steak with 1 tablespoon of the wine or sherry and stir-fry to separate the shreds.

2 Reduce the heat and pour off any excess liquid, then continue to stir-fry the meat gently until it is dry. Add the chilli bean paste, hoisin sauce, garlic, salt, sugar and remaining wine or sherry. Stir-fry for 1 minute.

3 Increase the heat, add the carrots and stir-fry for 2 minutes. Add the spring onions, ginger, Szechuan or black pepper and chilli oil, and stir to mix the ingredients. Serve immediately.

2 tablespoons sesame oil

300 g (10 oz) frying steak, cut into short fine strips

2 tablespoons Chinese wine or dry sherry

1 tablespoon chilli bean paste

1 tablespoon hoisin sauce

1 garlic clove, finely chopped

½ teaspoon salt

1 tablespoon sugar

125 g (4 oz) carrots, cut into short fine strips

2 spring onions, finely chopped

2 slices of fresh root ginger, peeled and finely chopped

½ teaspoon freshly ground Szechuan or black pepper

1 teaspoon chilli oil

Serves 4

Preparation time: 20–25 minutes

Cooking time: 15 minutes

beef with broccoli

1 In a bowl, mix together the oyster sauce, sherry and cornflour. Add the beef slices, turn to coat, cover and leave to marinate in the refrigerator for about 20 minutes.

2 If using dried mushrooms, drain and squeeze dry, discard the stalks and finely slice the caps.

3 Heat half of the oil in the wok. Add the beef slices and stir-fry for 10–15 seconds. Remove with a slotted spoon and set aside.

4 Heat the remaining oil, then add the ginger and spring onions, mushrooms, broccoli, bamboo shoots and carrot. Add the salt and sugar and stir-fry for 1½ minutes. Add the beef, stir well and moisten with a little water. Heat through and serve hot.

2 tablespoons oyster sauce

1 tablespoon dry sherry

1 tablespoon cornflour

250 g (8 oz) beef steak, cut into thickish slices

125 g (4 oz) button mushrooms or 3–4 Chinese dried mushrooms, soaked in warm water for 20 minutes

4 tablespoons vegetable oil

2 slices fresh root ginger, peeled and chopped

2 spring onions, chopped

175 g (6 oz) broccoli florets

125 g (4 oz) bamboo shoots, sliced

1 carrot, sliced

1 teaspoon salt

1 teaspoon sugar

Serves 4

Preparation time: 15 minutes, plus marinating

Cooking time: 5 minutes

1 tablespoon sunflower oil

1 onion, thinly sliced

1 garlic clove, crushed

375 g (12 oz) lean frying steak, cut into fine strips or small slices

2–3 plums, pitted and sliced

3 flat mushrooms, sliced

1 tablespoon Chinese wine or dry sherry

2 teaspoons soft brown sugar

1 tablespoon dark soy sauce

2 teaspoons cornflour

2 tablespoons water

2 spring onions, green part only, chopped, to garnish

1 Heat the oil in a wok or large frying pan. Add the onion and fry for 2 minutes. Stir in the garlic and steak, and stir-fry over a high heat for 2 minutes.

2 Reduce the heat and add the plums and mushrooms. Continue to stir-fry for 1 minute, then stir in the wine or sherry, sugar and soy sauce.

3 Blend the cornflour to a smooth paste with the water add this mixture to the pan, stirring until the sauce has thickened. Garnish with chopped spring onion and serve.

Serves 4
Preparation time: 6 minutes
Cooking time: 8 minutes

stir-fried beef with plum sauce & mushrooms

■ Plums add fragrant, fruity sweetness and a succulent contrast in texture to this attractive and hearty beef dish.

1 Blend the cornflour to a smooth paste with the soy sauce in a large bowl. Add the steak and turn it in the cornflour mixture to coat all the shreds. Cover and leave to marinate for 10 minutes.

2 Heat 2 tablespoons of the oil in a wok or large frying pan over a high heat. Stir-fry the steak for about 1 minute or until lightly browned. Remove with a slotted spoon and set aside.

3 Heat the remaining oil in the wok and stir-fry the beans with salt to taste for 1–1½ minutes. Replace the meat and stir in the wine or sherry with a little stock or water.

4 Reheat briefly until the ingredients are combined and the steak is hot. Do not overcook the mixture – the beans should be crisp and the meat tender. Add salt to taste and serve immediately, garnished with shredded spring onion.

fried beef with french beans

1 tablespoon cornflour

2 tablespoons light soy sauce

250 g (8 oz) lean frying steak, cut into short fine strips

4 tablespoons sunflower oil

250 g (8 oz) French beans, cut into 5 cm (2 inch) lengths

1 tablespoon Chinese wine or dry sherry

1–2 tablespoons beef stock or water

salt

shredded spring onion, to garnish

Serves 4

Preparation time: 15 minutes, plus marinating

Cooking time: 5 minutes

stir-fried liver & spinach

1 Blanch the liver in boiling water for a few seconds. Drain well and coat with cornflour.

2 Heat 2 tablespoons of the oil in a wok or large frying pan. Add the spinach and the salt, and stir-fry for 2 minutes. Arrange the spinach around the edge of a warmed serving dish, then set aside to keep hot.

3 Wipe the wok clean with kitchen paper and heat the remaining oil until very hot. Add the ginger, liver, soy sauce and wine or sherry. Stir-fry briskly for about 1–2 minutes, taking care not to over-cook the liver or it will become tough.

4 Pour the mixture into the middle of the spinach and garnish with spring onion. Serve immediately.

375 g (12 oz) pig's liver, cut into thin triangular slices

2 tablespoons cornflour

4 tablespoons sunflower oil

500 g (1 lb) spinach, washed and drained

1 teaspoon salt

2 thin slices of fresh root ginger, peeled

1 tablespoon light soy sauce

1 tablespoon Chinese wine or dry sherry

shredded spring onion, to garnish

Serves 4

Preparation time: 10 minutes

Cooking time: 3–4 minutes

stir-fried beef in hot chilli sauce

1 Season the steak with salt. Heat the oil in a wok or large frying pan over a moderate heat and fry the dried red chillies for 1 minute to flavour the oil. Use a slotted spoon to remove and discard the chillies.

2 Increase the heat, then stir-fry the steak for 1 minute until all the pieces are browned.

3 Add the garlic, ginger and spring onions, and cook for 30 seconds. Stir in the soy sauces, wine or sherry and green chillies, and cook for a further 1 minute.

4 Transfer to a warmed serving dish and serve immediately.

500 g (1 lb) rump steak, thinly sliced across the grain

2 tablespoons sunflower oil

2 dried red chillies

2 garlic cloves, sliced

2.5 cm (1 inch) piece of fresh root ginger, peeled and shredded

4 spring onions, shredded

2 tablespoons dark soy sauce

2 tablespoons light soy sauce

2 tablespoons Chinese wine or dry sherry

2 green chillies, deseeded and chopped

salt

Serves 4

Preparation time: 20 minutes

Cooking time: 4–5 minutes

■ Chinese rice wine is used in cooking, especially in sauces and marinades. It is suitable for drinking as well.

index